SONNETS

SONNETS

R. D. Laing

LONDON
MICHAEL JOSEPH

First published in Great Britain by Michael Joseph Ltd
44 Bedford Square, London WC1B 3EF
1979
© 1979 R. D. Laing

ISBN 0 7181 1822 7

Typeset and printed in Great Britain by
Ebenezer Baylis & Son Limited
The Trinity Press, Worcester, and London
and bound by
Hunter and Foulis Ltd, Edinburgh

1

Is it our proper destiny to spurn
The mortal vessel of our frail desire?
To drench our flame in flame and so expire
In pure, white, cold, dead ash, and then to burn
To naught the final dross until all's lost?
We moths may be mistaken. Not thus
May we awaken from the evil curse
Of spirit blighted in a fiery frost.

Amor and *caritas*, as one, surpass
The impasse of their severed discontent.
No fragrant token of their immanent
Atonement wafts from transcendental ash.

We learn to reconcile the high and low
In consummation's warm and gentle glow.

2

Content and form must aptly fit the thought.
The pulse of life must animate the whole.
There must be not one dead superfluous spot.
It must all burn. There can be cold coal.

Signification, sensibility
Should sing their counterpoint throughout each line.
The order of the wildest rhapsody
Should tune the heart, refresh the tired mind.

We can't expect to grasp the total truth
Of forest fire, earthquake and avalanche.
Nature and man can both be so uncouth,
And the most mediocre also dance.

Not every discord deigns to harmonize,
And beauty is not always true or wise.

3

Ah yes. The discipline that gives the air
Of freedom to the beckonings of chance.
The strictures of the tightly measured dance
Obeyed, achieved, enjoyed, may dare
Suggest a way of bedding fair with fair
Where each, as each, can only both enhance:
A way whereby all elements romance
In lucid joyful song beyond despair.

Birds need obscure stars before they sing.
A world is in the simplest harmony.
We all are slaves. There is no queen or king
Who can dictate to sovereign destiny.
Nothing can more sure chastisement bring
Than contradicting bland necessity.

4

When I consider what you mean to me,
It is a fact I've come to realize
That you're my closest link to paradise
Despite what wise men try to make me see.

They caution us against idolatry
And tell us that we should not jeopardize
Immortal life for anything that dies:
And not to be bemused by mere beauty.

It seems ungracious not to take delight
In day because it turns so soon to night.
Eternity is always here to stay:
It's only you and I who fade away.

You are my here and now, my present tense.
I hope you will excuse my diffidence.

5

For Jutta

Will you reserve your next lifetime for me?
I'll try to fix it so we're snuggled in
A womb unfound by yet undreamt-of sin,
Oblivious to what we do not see.

We'll weave a skein around us from mankind,
Perpetually safe beyond disgrace
Within our indissolvable embrace,
Interminably, blissfully, entwined.

Perhaps, my love, we'll never meet again.
There is no price to pay. But I shall call
And you'll forget to answer: And be gay:
Until an echo steals upon your brain
To make you fancy you can just recall
How happy you once were with me today.

6

Love does not always find a way: but gives
A promise that it cannot be destroyed.
It's even killed and buried: yet it lives
In every heart in which it's crucified.

Love is sheer joy. But has to suffer you
And me. It can't avoid its Calvary.
Silent. Unseen. Transparent, pure and true,
Rich in its own reward of poverty.

When we can find us one to whom to turn,
On nothing but on it can we rely
To consume us, or else we can but burn
In just the fire we persecute it by.

Love cannot help but always wish all well.
Its denial is the essence of hell.

7

If only you would tell me that you love
Me still. Then I'd pretend I understood
You have to do your thing. Somewhere above
I'd find the strength to wish you your own good.

Don't think you can dispense with flattery.
Don't think I cannot even up the score.
You do not have a shred of generosity.
Can't you who's such a liar, tell one more?

It doesn't cost the earth to keep me sweet,
And better far for you than if I'm sour.
You only have to say that when we meet
You cannot live or breathe, but for that hour.

You'll be rewarded more than you can guess
If you will help disguise my callousness.

8

I want you happy, beautiful and free.
You can have everything you want and more,
As long as you don't say that it's a chore
To spend your life entirely with me.

I cannot hear the voice of charity.
But sometimes on an empty, windswept shore,
Like rusty hinges on a cellar door,
I've heard the creakings of self-mockery.

I just can't bring myself to contemplate
That maybe you are not as you appear
To me. I've even felt the pangs of doubt
That if you had your chance to choose your mate
I would not be the one that you'd hold dear.
Don't speak. Forgive me. I must not find out.

9

Why don't you keep it to yourself? You think
That all you have to do is let it all
Hang out. You'll never find your missing link
By your ridiculous love-call.

It may make *you* feel better, but you don't
Connect with me. You only aggravate
Our situation by the fact you won't
Realize I much prefer to masturbate

Than to make love with you. The only way
To make me want to want you as before
Is to convince me that you'll not betray
A trust your lies have rotted to the core.

The past is gone and I am left forlorn.
Hatred's not dead and love's not yet born.

10

If she did not love you, she would not be
Jealous. I wish you would appreciate
A little more, how justified she is to hate.
You locked the door and threw away the key.
Don't try to tell me, that I cannot see
She does not own you. She's your chosen mate.
And you yourself should know the married state
Is not a contract, but a mystery.

I am not now the man I was before.
I'm sorry I don't like her any more.
What right have you to ask me to pretend
That all desire for her's not at an end?
The unexpected movements of one's soul
Arise completely out of one's control.

11

I never thought that you'd make love to me.
I never dreamt to live and taste such wine.
But now my joy has turned to agony
And gall. For I am yours, but you're not mine.

I know that there are other lips, of course, to kiss.
I'm not the only thing that makes you sing.
I sense that when with me, you yet may miss
The raptures others, no doubt, sometimes bring.

My jealousy is not hung out for show.
So please in turn do this for me: be kind.
About your sins, I do not want to know.
As your penance, spare my peace of mind.

I still can feel some pleasure through the pain.
But be discreet. Or even that will wane.

I did not want to fall in love with you.
But I'm not free. Even the air can't choose.
The day of my release is overdue.
You are a need I can afford to lose.

Don't say you never asked me to. I don't
Blame you. Why not admit you like the thought
That I will give you all you want
If you will never say your love is bought?

Although I wish that we had never met,
I cannot let you dream of going away:
And don't be ever tempted to forget
To go on lying in the same old way.

I hope we never live through this again.
I cannot bear to hear you say: Amen.

13

Is this indeed our last, our final kiss?
Is this how all these timeless moments end?
It isn't easy to realize, my friend,
That we no longer are each other's bliss.

Regrets we shall eventually dismiss.
Our broken hearts, probably, will mend.
It should not tax the hardened fates to send
Us futures no more dim than this.

The past does not presume to tell us why
Our wildest raptures can become so tame.

How many deaths are we required to die
Before we find the way to play the game?

Perhaps there's consolation in the sigh
That cannot find the whom or what to blame.

14

She's gone. All gone. I should have kissed her more.
But now. Too late. I'm left with wretched might –
Have-beens and helpless yesterdays, a store
Of what can never ever be set right.

I should have held her closer, told her, shown
Her that she was my ecstasy. But all
I did was play the fool and act the clown.
I could not see the writing on the wall.

It's over now, but for those silent wails
Echoing through the unforgiving nights.
No use to itemize regrets for tales
Of filthy lies. We could have scaled the heights

But. There it is. Don't make the same mistake.
Don't prevaricate. Give your heart a break.

15

We lost ourselves in love.
                        And then lost love.
We searched for it through both our hearts.
                                    In vain.
We found only our graves.
                        We looked above,
Below, about:
                but always the same pain.

The pain has gone   We sit and watch TV
We seldom yawn   She makes me cups of tea
We tell no tales   There's no more need
                                for guile
We do not pick our nails   We sometimes smile.

We're grateful to the powers that be
For lifeless, loveless, hateless, apathy

I can't remember when I last felt glad
I can't remember when I last felt sad

I can't remember when I last got pissed
I can't remember when I last was kissed.

16

Now all our guests have come and gone away,
And you and I can hold each other close.
No need for haste as we await the day
The night falls into. No need suppose
We've failed to find what we had lost before
We caught the gleam in one another's eyes
Which signalled hope returned, to teach us more
Than seemed our crumpled hearts could realize.

  The ghosts of youth are weary of the stage.
There's no one left to offer us a fight.
No sermons we must sit through at our age.
No passing fancies shrouding our delight.
Sweetheart, our love is true, but can't outlast
Our ruined, raddled flesh. O hold me fast.

17

I cannot say that I'm the man that I
Once was. He slaved away to set me free.
He left a nice soft bed on which to lie
To whom he'd be when he had reached eighty.

He did the sowing. I reap what was sown.
He picked and pressed the grapes. I drink the wine.
I still am paying interest on his loan.
I am the legacee of his design.

The wings of youth can't help the legs of age
To totter on toward the final trial.
Whatever is the writing on the final page
I'm what's come out of all those years' denial.
I ask myself if he would be happy
If he could know he's turned out to be me.

18

Another one won't do me any harm.
The damage is already long since done.
I'm nothing now I've lost my funky charm.
There's no one left who knows last time I won.

There's no doubt if I alcoholize my brain
It's somehow not so bad, but still the same.
And with a little more, I can't refrain
From following my customary game.

Perhaps I'm after all not *depassé*.
Who knows. I still might have it in me yet.
The best is yet to be. I know a way
To make a million dead. You want a bet?

It's time to have another round, what think?
Hey, Hullo, baby! Come here! Have a drink!

19

You once were lean, but now you're fat.
Now you've achieved your trivial success,
It does not seem to matter to you that
You're a complete and utter mess.

Don't think that no one's seen the games you play.
Your victories are triumphs of defeat.
There're some can smell the rank decay
Within your rotten soul. You vicious cheat.

There with the grace of God you go. More cruel
Than I can ever dare to formulate
A wish to be. You stand up proud and well,
A tare for other tares to emulate.

I do not like to think that your façade
Could be the image of myself gone bad.

20

Graduation Address

We want to help you keep your innocence
As long as possible. Not just because
We want you to believe in Santa Claus.
Or even to imagine that your life makes sense.

We're not naïve. It's simple self-defence.
If you always obey our God-sent laws,
And never once suspect their many flaws,
You'll never look to us for recompense.

We simply had to have it understood,
Beyond all proof, that you are bad and we are good.
We simply had to compromise your mind
To save being cruel, and to be kind.

You need not worry about destiny.
You are deep-programmed machinery.

21

Presidential Candidate

What have you got to say to the American
People in thirty seconds flat? Hullo.
We're still the strongest nation. We began
So recently and have so far to go.

We've hardly started yet. We are a great
Adventure. And the land of hope for all
Who think and feel that mankind needs a state
Of freedom and of justice to recall

Ourselves to what we can achieve
When we are not afraid, defending or
Attacking, poor or hungry. We believe
In God, and shall bring peace to earth.
Let "Onward, upward" be our battle cry.
I thank you for your kind attention. Bye.

I used to be a decent woman. Then I met
The man I loved and I became his wife.
It was so pleasant not to have to sweat
Away the ordinary hours of life.

I liked to shop and buy the children clothes.
We liked to cuddle tight throughout the night.
When he came home I helped him warm his toes.
All right. Then suddenly he lost his sight.

There's someone to be with him through the day
While I go on the street. We have to eat.
The council thought the children best away.
They're learning quickly how to bleat.

Thank Thee, O Lord, for Thy Divine Mercy.
He cannot see what Thou hast done to me.

23

Sometimes I think it is a rotten deal
For human kind to have to live within
This flesh and reconcile itself to feel
Its dissolution and eventual ruin.

I'm grateful to have got thus far.
May what's to come be not too fraught with pain.
I'll bless the Lord and thank each lucky star,
If I don't have to be Abel or Cain.

A painless, healthy, happy, comfy death
Is not presumptuous at least to ask.
I hope brutality and ugliness
Be not what lingers on my mask.

The pen slips out of icy finger-tips.
No words of wisdom come from dead men's lips.

24

First we start showing signs of wear and tear
And no more feel like rolling in the snow.
Then we begin to realize that we're
Senescent and have not long to go.

Are we aware we cannot remember who
We are? Does it require great fortitude
To live *a*taxic and *a*phasic through
An *un*-anaesthesized decrepitude?

And yet there are some very very old
And frail creatures who look content and glad
To be just where they're at. Their ha nds are cold.
They've almost shed the life that they once had.

The one unmitigated blessing of old age
Is that, soon, soon, the bird will leave the cage.

25

Some say they know the reason why
We're here. And others with an equal force
Insist, their voices no less harsh and hoarse,
That nothing's true. It's all a primal lie.

When we begin to wrangle and dispute
Over what's past our discernment,
We're merely idiots who have not learnt
The mind can't see or know the Absolute.

The wisest man's still just a man. The one
Who knows himself a fool has grace
To see he sees *his* glaikit* image on
The hidden glory of *His* unseen Face.

On Judgement Day there's nothing to discuss.
Let's hope and pray that God believes in us.

* unreflectively self-satisfied.

26

Man's inhumanity to man remains
A puzzle unresolved. Perhaps we should
Know why we are so bad at being good.
Our purest thoughts are thick with bloody stains
Of all the lives that have been shed to give
Us life to think them. We bear the scars
Of massacres our forebears wrought; of wars
They won with rapes and tortures. History's sieve
Has left us here, selected to elect
Ourselves elected to perpetuate
The race until the gods eliminate
Our kind, for reasons we shall not detect.
It's strange to feel such twinges of regret
For unlived lives of those we've never met.

27

My friend insists he needs a bayonet's
Point pressing in between his ribs to make
Him come alive. It justifies him, whets
His appetite. Affords a welcome break

From guilt. If not in danger, then
There must be somewhere he must have gone wrong.
An honest man is socially barren
If he is not a menace to the strong.

For him to sing and dance would be perverse.
He'd be ashamed to dream of being at peace

As long as all his brothers can't converse
Unbothered by the bandits or police.

Pleasure's a self-indulgent luxury
He grudges all relief from misery.

28

Thank God for when even a privileged few
Can breathe without the choice of loss of life
Or pitiful abjection to the crew
Who've learned to argue with the carving knife.

No one's been given any guarantee
That every dogma has to coalesce,
What's on for you may well be off for me,
It may be either or, not more or less

We must remember never to forget –
We *must* be wrong, however we were right,
If good intentions give the nudge to set
The world ablaze to fire it with our light.

Yes! All infinities are summed in One.
Spare us the mathematics of the gun.

29

How can I help my fellow man, and make
A contribution to the commonweal,
If I am bound to make the old mistake
Of taking false for true, fictions for real?

The wise man leaves the world. You can't be more
Compassionate than take the robe and bowl.
In setting off to reach the further shore
You illustrate in action man's right goal.

My delusion is that I think we're all
Deluded. Whatever I am going to find
Will have to be another comical
Invention of my self-mistrustful mind.

Be calm. No thoughts. Talk is a useless bore.
And silence is another metaphor?

30

You tell us that it's by faith alone
(Itself a gift of grace) we can be saved.
By our own efforts, we cannot atone
For mortal sin. Even the best behaved

Is guilty of the crucifixion. We've
No right to expect mercy. Bow down. All
In Adam die. A few in Christ revive
Who are elected to receive His call.

There's nothing we can do. If we do not
Believe we perish if we don't believe,
We perish. Either God or Satan's got
Us in His power since Adam and Eve.

We can't prevent ourselves being mortified:
And get no credit if we're justified.

31

I wonder how you are encumbered by
No metaphysical uncertainty.
You're saved from the temptation of the lie
That says we're lost in our own misery.

To you damnation and salvation
Are not merely products of the human soul.
No evil has the power to debar
The power of God to make us Whole.

I hope it's not *my* fault *I'm* such a fool
As not to know whether He is or not:
Or if it's by His Grace that we are grateful
Or if I've lost or found the truth I sought.

Maybe nothing is all we need to know,
But if it is, O Lord, please tell us so.

32

No one but me can hear the mental din
Of clashing thoughts and images that fight
A bloodless, ghostly fight to determine
Which hordes of phantoms have the right
To a monopoly of me. I am
A would-be refugee from any kind
Of violence. But here I'm in a jam.
I'm motionlessly fleeing from my mind.

I'm devastated by a dreary war
That may be only manure from my brain.
But it goes on. I can't remember what it's for.
There's none to whom I dare complain.

A precise cut with my sharp, gentle knife
Is all you need to end this pointless strife.

33

Polonius

The freedom you desire is in the mean
Between opposing tensions in your soul.
Achieve the integration of the whole
And then you *are*, and not a *might*-have-been.

Remember that to live is to metabolize.
So don't forget en route to the sublime
To check on your mouth-anus transit time.
Look at the ground as well as at the skies.

You've heard it all before? That's fine.
Reiterated truths soon sound absurd.
To be blasé is not beatitude.
It's just your glutted tongue can't taste the wine.
One in a million hears the blatant word
Before its echoes into platitude.

34

Socrates

He taught us what we do not want to know:
That what we think we know we seldom do:
That what we know we seldom know we know.
Sagacity's the mark of very few.

He called himself a midwife. He aimed
To ask the questions not to answer them.
With arrogant humility he claimed
An ignorance men still condemn.

Those enigmatic shadows on the cave
Are not whatever casts them. He believed
He loved the Truth so much he had to save
Her from the stain of anything conceived.

The cure for life's a boon we can't refuse,
For death's the gift of Aesculapius.

35

If He exists, it's only through His Grace
That He's so far away or awfully near.
We would be blinded if we glimpsed His Face.
He choses those to whom He tells He's here.

If He exists, through Him alone arc we devout
And bask under the sun of certitude.
His will alone impels in us the doubt
That He's all powerful, all knowing, all good.

We can but beg. If He decides to starve
Us, we can only carry on until we rot.
And if He's not, then still we have to carve
A chunk of meaning out of what we've got.

It's funny, were it not ridiculous,
To ask: Did we make Him, or He make us?

36

It's all correct, and crisp, and keen and bright.
A place of order, form and right design.
A haven, in this world of dark, of light,
A Where to start a long and clean straight line.

It would be nice if all around we saw .
The grace, decorum of the antique mind
Brought forward to the present as a law,
Instead of our cacophonous and brutal bind.

It should not need to hearten me so much
To come across a little worth, among
The slosh and drivel, dross and mulch
Which would be better formed of honest dung.

The falling leaves are harbingers of spring
The game's not up. Some children still can sing.

37

There's light and love and joy and freshness yet.
There're those who have something to celebrate.
There can be times we hope we'll not forget.
A helping hand is not always too late.

Up really high there's still clear perfect blue.
Morning must dawn as long as there is night.
Without the old there's nothing to renew.
Once in a while it almost feels all right.

Although I know that light needs dark to shine,
I don't expect to tell what atoms mean.
The universe is fine without being mine.
The flowers of countless valleys grow unseen.

What is above subsists on what's beneath.
The world is not entirely blasted heath.

38

To *live* our life's the grand adventure: fit
For any hero. Nothing else can be
The meaning of our absurd mystery.
We'd like to think that there's some benefit
Somewhere, to something, someone, to the All,
That we're such sacks of comic lust: or good
For us that we are thus.

                     At least we're food
For worms. However spirit fail, the call
Of death's a reconciliation for
Our flesh, *its* contribution to the feast
Which we partake of. Eater eaten, beast
For beast. From dust to dust. No less, no more.

We can be sure of death's utility,
However much of life's but vanity.

To write a sonnet in this day and age
May seem to some an almost wanton waste
Of ink upon a page. Yet still we rage
Or rave, lament or praise, in haste
To make our present offering to the sun
Before our time, too long, too short, is done.

The chub-chub-chubbing of our throbbing heart
Will some day stop. And then? And then we know
Not what awaits us as we end, and start
To find the start, or end, of all this flow.
Then, twenty, seconds after our last breath,
Shall we be wiser, or be nil, with death?

Adages

Wilt thou be wise, my son.
At the knees of a woman begin.
Her eyes shall teach thee thy road
The worth of the thing called folly,
The joy of the thing called sin.
Else shalt thou go to thy grave in pain
For the folly that might have been.
                    'The Wisdom of Merlin'
                    Wilfred Scawen Blunt

There is no joy in sin, but there may be joy in the thing called sin. Sexual desire is not evil in itself. Yes indeed it is spiritually perilous. That is not a threat, but a warning. Take care, and love, with you.

Nay, let us walk from fire to fire,
From passionate pain to deadlier delight,
I am too young to live without desire.
Too young art thou to waste this summer night.

Yes. Yet it is a shame that desire is so often so ruthless.

The satisfaction of desire may not be wrong, if it does not entail the betrayal of love; if neither takes advantage of the other; if no one is trespassing; if there is no deceit involved: no exploitation, no revenge, no callous, casual conception of a new being, already foredoomed to be killed.

You are making love. Are you making friends?

The sweetest thing in all the world is to love and to be loved in return.

To desire and to love, and to be desired and to be loved in return, unreservedly, with no impediments of any kind, is, without doubt, one of the sweetest experiences of living.

The test of the quality of our love may come only when we find ourselves loving and desiring, without being loved or desired in return; or even being desired, but do not desire; or when circumstances thwart the reciprocal gratification of desire.

Then desire is liable to lose its sweetness. As the wine turns to vinegar, as desire becomes sour and bitter, does what we thought was love become also soured and embittered? Does it alter when it alteration finds? Do we crash from the rosy glow of beneficence, and become resentful, revengeful, spiteful, malicious and mean?

Does such tribulation make us nicer or nastier? wiser? or merely sadder and badder?

That is the test.

It has been said: *He who most doubts his love, loves the best.*

Love is rigorous. The question is whether it is out of love, on behalf of love, for love's sake, that we dread to confuse the sweet pleasure of getting what one wants, or the pain of not getting what one wants, with the joy or suffering of Love.

The final sin of man is his unwillingness to concede he is a sinner.

Luther

The deeper we are in sin, the less we imagine we are sinful. Sin is a double ignorance: an ignorance of ignorance.

Lead us not into temptation but deliver us from evil.

What a terrifying, what a sobering and salutary thought! That it is by God's will that we are led into temptation or delivered from evil.

Every virtue has its evil double. Fallen angels may sing in perfect counterpoint.

In a sense, we find ourselves only in losing ourselves. But we may lose ourselves without finding ourselves.

Credulity is not faith. Illusion is not hope. Narcissism is not self-love. Moths make mistakes, but the ruthless angels of cold daybreaks know how to preserve their chastity. Our lamentations do not prove we care.

We do not exonerate ourselves from guilt merely by causing pain to others by our cruel confessions. We do not cease to be guilty because we plead guilty. We do not prove a love of truth merely by spreading around the vilest libels and slanders about others, or equally about ourselves, just because they are true. Facts are often foul. Love alone knows when to speak, or be silent.

47

We should practise what we preach; and it may be humility, or cowardice, or an over-scrupulous, a too exquisitely fastidious tact that prompts us not to preach what we practise.

Lord forgive us for we know not what we do.

The self which condemns itself is the last to realize that it is not only the self it condemns that stands in need of forgiveness, but the self that condemns.

How difficult it is to realize that our very righteousness is as filthy rags!

The thought that God can and may wash our rags, filthy with the righteousness we acquire each day in keeping clean, is an offence to our prideful sense of guilt. We want to feel righteous rather than that God in His mercy may be forgiving even our righteousness.

Goodness perishes with evil, unless both are redeemed. Goodness cannot save evil, no more can it save itself.

It is evil if it thinks it can.

Everyone should be careful not to set himself as his aim.
attributed to Rabbi Mendel of Kotzk

Some people pursue what they take to be their own enlightenment, or self-realization, or salvation, with an all-consuming greed, which they believe is a holy zeal. They are so avaricious that nothing can satisfy them. They do not want more of this and that, they want more *consciousness* of this and that. They take it as a virtue that nothing is good enough for them, not even God. They are not good enough for themselves, so they pant for more goodness. They love the truth if it is more cruel than lies. They pride themselves with their own indifference to anything except their own spiritual ambitions. As they despise more they want less, and want to want less and less, in order to feel more and more above beyond it all. They confuse their callousness for the non-attachment of charity, and their attachment to their own self-contempt for humility, which inflames their sense of their own superiority.

They love to quote:

If any man come to me, and hate not his father, and mother, and wife, and children, and brethren, and sisters, yea, and his own life also, he cannot be my disciple.

Luke 14:26

They relish the prospect, or the memory, of emulating the Buddha as he gallops off on his white horse, abandoning his wife and son the moment his son was born.

These people long to meet the Buddha or God incarnate, coming along the road, in the *hope* that He will get in their way, just for the chance to kill Him – and so to preen themselves at being so spiritually advanced.

We can do what we will. But we cannot will as we will.

Nietzsche

No man is free.
There are those who are neither the slaves of man, or woman, nor are they the slaves of God.
They fancy themselves to be free men.
They are the slaves of the devil.

Can a man who has looked into his own soul really respect himself?

Dostoevsky

This is one of those questions it is prudent not to answer. If one answers 'Yes', one is open to the charges of, at best, naïvety, at worst, profound self-deception. If one says 'No', a chorus of self-respectful voices immediately shout, 'Speak for yourself!'

It takes a wise man to ask such a question; only a fool would dare to risk answering it.

There are people who are constantly at the ready to take advantage of others. If you know too much, for them you are suspect. How could you, unless you are tainted with madness or have looked further into evil than any good man should? Or, if they think you know too little, or are wrong, God help you if they get you in their power. Apart from the peril of perdition, the gravest risk most of us encounter is to be at the mercy of other human beings.

Goethe is credited with a remark to the effect that: it is said that we get wiser as we grow older, but the truth is that it is difficult to remain as wise as once we were.

This is the sort of remark which one is best to keep to oneself when young, for then it will be taken for arrogance. Reserve it for old age, when it will be more likely to be admired, especially by the young, who do not know any better, for the modesty of seasoned wisdom. The only people in a position to evaluate it at its true worth can be discounted. They will be dead soon anyway.

We have been recommended to pray: *Forgive us our trespasses, as we forgive them that trespass against us.*

We may mistake an action for a trespass when it is not. We may fail to recognize a trespass for what it is.

There are those who will go to incredible lengths not to realize they are being trespassed against.

They are frightened lest they be unable to forgive, because if they cannot find it in their hearts to forgive others how can they then expect God to forgive them? Hence they try to convince themselves that no one is trespassing against them, so that they will have nothing to forgive.

Am I entitled to pray: Forgive me for not forgiving those that trespass against me? It certainly takes a lot of nerve.

Here lie I, Martin Elginbroddie.
Hae mercy on my soul, Lord God:
As I wad do, were I Lord God,
And ye were Martin Elginbroddie.

Sometimes I forgive and remember.
Sometimes I forgive and forget.
Sometimes I neither forgive nor forget.
Sometimes I do not forgive? and forget.

It is infuriating to hold something against someone and not to be able to remember what it is.

We should not settle into a complacent smugness at the thought of being one's own worst enemy. That is no virtue. Why not be one's own best friend? Or at least treat oneself no worse than one treats one's neighbour?

There are those who suffer the sins of others better than they do their own. They do not so much forgive others as pretend that there is nothing to forgive. But when it comes to themselves, they do not even want to bother God by being so self-indulgent as to pray for their own forgiveness.

I cannot turn the other cheek, unless I realize I have been hit on one. But whether I turn the other cheek or not, it does not do my neighbour any good to give him the impression that he is not trespassing against me if he is.

There are those, often mistaken for masochists, who are so sorry for the one who is doing them in that they cannot bring themselves to defend themselves. They may even feel that they cannot love the one who is abusing them, if they allow themselves to see that they are being abused.

Love is not always blind. It may see just enough – to prefer the dark.

There are those who, finding nothing in men and women worthy of love, dedicate themselves to the service of humanity. I wish they would not. But nothing can stop them scourging us, undeserving humanity, with their terrible dedication. In their loveless service to what they despise, they are prepared, with no hint of compunction, to inflict on us any amount of pain, havoc and death, to destroy the present, to make way for their future.

And Jesus went out, and his disciples, into the towns of Caesarea Philippi: and by the way he asked his disciples, saying unto them, Whom do men say that I am?
And they answered, John the Baptist: but some say, Elias; and others, One of the prophets.
And he saith unto them, But whom say ye that I am?
And Peter answereth and saith unto him, Thou art the Christ.
And he charged them that they should tell no man of him.

Mark 8:27–30

Who, what, whence, whither, why am I, are perhaps questions which, although we cannot not ask, we cannot answer.

If Jesus was very God of very God incarnate in man, as a man, with a human mind as well as a human body, perhaps, as a man, he did not ordinarily know who he was, any more than, ordinarily, he walked on water.

Perhaps he did not himself know who he was.

Blessed are the poor in spirit.

None of us possess the spirit. There is no way to own it. No way to invest it, or in it. No way to acquire spiritual capital. No way to control it. No way to use it. The moment we try to use it, we are the bondslaves of evil. Perfect freedom is in total service to it. But there is no way of press-ganging ourselves into its service. It may or may not choose us. It may or may not use us. Spiritual gifts are granted or withheld to rich and poor alike, the apparently deserving and the apparently undeserving.

The joyful tribulation of abject spiritual poverty teaches us the essential lesson that our daily spiritual bread is not baked by us. Nothing is, could be or should be clearer. Spiritual beggars are blessed with this luminous certainty.

Thy will be done on earth as it is in Heaven.

Apparently it is *not* being done on earth as it is in Heaven, or else why should we be recommended to pray that it be done?

On behalf of the One that Evil crucifies, one may be tempted to lose faith in the Crucified One.

It is a curiously devious temptation to lose faith in the spirit because the spirit is crucified. It is a curious Mephistophelian sophistry to argue that nothing matters, because nothing matters or the wrong things matter for so many.

The evil heart hates Christ because He is crucified, because He is not Caesar; as it despises Caesar because He was assassinated. Nothing succeeds *but* success.

When we are so heavy hearted that we can't entirely believe in what we would like to believe, are we heavy hearted because we have lost faith in the Truth, or because we have lost hope in the Truth coming true?

We may become very downcast by being able to see only the way the Way, the Truth and the Life, is crucified in this world. Crucifixion without resurrection is the ultimate nightmare. It may or may not be love that makes us so sad or angry at all the nasty things that go on. But it is a mean betrayal of love to turn against it because it takes such a battering.

There are those who, having lost hope, try to turn their misfortune into a virtue. They affect to despise hope as trivial, cheap, dirty, as a stain on the pure shining steel of the implacable stoical soul.

Of course, hope may be petty, false, evil, corrupt. But we fall into a crude error if we turn against hope as such, a God-given gift, by confusing it with the very state of illusion we *hope*, surely, we all may be delivered from.

Spiritual comfort comes to us only through grace. In our disconsolation we may not be able to say we know it. But even if it has not come to us as a positive experience, its negative presence haunts us as the unseen evidence of faith, suffusing us with the burning necessity of hope, the final test of love.

For the reason and will which constitute God's essence must differ by the breadth of all heaven from our reason and will and have nothing in common with them except the name: as little, in fact, as the dog-star has in common with the dog, the barking animal.

Spinoza

It has been said that, to the philosopher, nothing he can unveil is permitted to veil itself. The theologian can afford to be the most avid of philosophers if, and only if, he already knows the mystery is a mystery, which no amount of the most reckless, abandoned intellectual depravity can unveil.

Scepticism, I have heard somewhere, is at best a kind of intellectual chastity.

We cannot understand even a grain of sand, let alone comprehend God.

It is only reasonable to realize that it is unreasonable to expect to be able to grasp with reason, or to form an image of, the very ground of the possibility of reason and imagination.

But to believe that what is totally beyond our reason and imagination is too absurd to credit is neither to credit nothing, nor to credit anything. It is sheer absurdity.

God is infinitely beyond our anthropomorphic, anthropocentric thoughts and images. Once we are thoroughly imbued with this realization, we may fall into the other arrogance of despising such homely images of the Divine mystery, couched in the sex and gender and drama of human kinship relations.

They are no more than a rattle to quieten a crying infant. Indeed, I am glad of a rattle. I do not need to throw it away to know it is a rattle.

The truth of every myth is an ineffable mystery, which cannot reveal its secrets to the outsider and cannot be uttered by the insider, and cannot be known to any knower, outsider or insider. In the Christian traditions, this has been stated for all traditions, once and for all, by Dionysius the Areopagite.

. . . He is neither soul nor intellect; nor has He imagination, opinion, reason or understanding; nor can He be expressed or conceived, since He is neither number, nor order; nor greatness, nor smallness; nor equality, nor inequality; nor similarity, nor dissimilarity; neither is He standing, nor moving, nor at rest; neither has He power, nor is power, nor

is light; neither does He live, nor is He life; neither is He essence, nor eternity, nor time; nor is He subject to intelligible contact; nor is He science, nor truth, nor kingship, nor wisdom; neither one, nor oneness; nor godhead, nor goodness; nor is He spirit according to our understanding, nor filiation, nor paternity; nor anything else known to us or to any other beings, of the things that are or the things that are not; neither does anything that is, know Him as He is; nor does He know existing things according to existing knowledge; neither can the reason attain to Him, nor name Him, nor know Him; neither is He darkness nor light, nor the false, nor the true; nor can any affirmation or negation be applied to Him, for although we may affirm or deny the things below Him, we can neither affirm nor deny Him, inasmuch as the all-perfect and unique Cause of all things transcends all affirmation, and the simple pre-eminence of His absolute nature is outside of every negation — free from every limitation and beyond them all.

I am the Resurrection and the life: whosoever believeth in me, though he were dead, yet shall he live; and whosoever liveth, and believeth in me, shall not die in eternity.

Canticle of Zacharias

In time, we die. The gift of God is death in time, and life in eternity.
The death through which we have to pass does not lie ahead of us in time.

Death is where we come to our end.

We cease to be captivated by death, only by realizing its reality.
The denial of death places us in its spell.
Deliverance from the spell of the death we deny is salvation.

The 'I' I take myself to be or know is, in a sense, always dead, since it is always an 'I was' that must always end, for me to *be*, now.

Bethlehem, Calvary are not only in the past. Our deliverance (not from the death of this body, but, in the expression of Saint Paul, from *the body of this death*, in which we perish with each passing moment) comes the Spirit which is now *and* always. We miss the point, we sin, as long as we imagine that there is anything to which to cling to save us from the need to cling.

The present, always so momentary, becomes truly momentous when *in* the moment, which takes no time at all, we find eternity.

Eternity is always here to stay
It's only you and I who fade away

The Christian message is the good news that life eternal is not at the far-off edge of time but is *in* time. The Kingdom – or more literally, the *Queen-dom* of Heaven – is *in* us.

Where two or three of us gather together in His Name, even just in the *name* of the Way, the Truth and the Life, there the only I AM is, that ever was or shall be, Very God of Very God, Jesus Christ Our Lord, in our very midst—— free from all our limitations and beyond us all. Amen?